LIGHT SLEEPER

Coleman Stevenson

Light Sleeper: Poems

Copyright © Coleman Stevenson, 2020

All rights reserved.

ISBN 978-1-949127-14-0

First edition

Edited by Ariel Kusby & Bobby Eversmann

Book design by Mickey Collins

Cover image: *Untitled (Blue), 2017* by Lucia Volker

Published by Deep Overstock, Portland, OR.

deepoverstock.com

**DEEP OVERSTOCK
PUBLISHING**

LIGHT SLEEPER

Table of Contents

Household Gods

The Accidental Rarefication of Pattern #5609	12
If you were nearby you'd be singing.	38
Loved Them Like Snow	41
Hunters	43
Ask Me	44
Year of Dead Dogs	46
Tell me spring is not	48
The Flowerwaterers	52
The Enigma of Arrival	53
The Problem with Metaphysics	54
Mystery and Melancholy of a Street	56
Explanations/Excuses	58
The Unfair Hours	59
Nasturtiums	60
Nothing at All or Everything at Once	67

Counting Across a Finite Field

In the world of sea monkeys, each undulation makes a wave.	70
Before It Was This	71
I Only Wanted You For Your Warmth	73
The Tilting Horizon Over the World Full of Holes	74
The Path & the Obstacle	76
Penance	80
What am I not giving you that you need?	82
It Takes Me by Surprise	83
The Light and the Clouds Came In	84
St. Clare rifles through a pile of receipts.	86
St. Clare is nourished by the mere elements.	87
St. Clare takes her Orders.	89
St. Clare talks to The Cross.	90
St. Clare does the laundry, folds the sheets like flags.	91
St. Clare cleans the house for company.	92
St. Clare admits: Our bodies are not made of brass.	93
St. Clare questions the tether of spirit to relic.	94

    Life   95
    A Sudden Swerve   98

Feathers and Lead

    I Am Nothing's Mother   100
    Seven Days   102
    The Cinnabar Fields   106
    Who will not run?   108
    Museum of Glass & Bone   110
    Monsters   116
    Cannot Be Sustained   118
    Everything Is Red   120
    Couldn't Say, and Didn't: Part 1   121
    Couldn't Say, and Didn't: Part 2   122
    Couldn't Say, and Didn't: Part 3   123
    Couldn't Say, and Didn't: Part 4   124
    Couldn't Say, and Didn't: Part 5   126
    Couldn't Say, and Didn't: Part 6   127
    Couldn't Say, and Didn't: Part 7   128
    Couldn't Say, and Didn't: Part 8   130
    Couldn't Say, and Didn't: Part 9   131
    The End of Change   132
    This Is What the Morning Is   136

Index   138
Acknowledgement/Notes   143

my heart a fist
my tongue a key
my head a crown

Household Gods

The Accidental Rarefication of Pattern #5609

> So long as we love life for itself we seldom dread the losing it. When we desire life for the attainment of an object, we recognize the frailty of its texture.
>
> — Nathaniel Hawthorne, "The Artist of the Beautiful"

> ...I buried the frog because it was dead
> and dug it up because I'd been dreaming...
>
> — Robert Wrigley, "The Afterlife"

1. How do you know what to keep?

When I was a girl, acorns were olives with hats, and gravel lay in the road like diamonds to be mined. Mine, a childhood not full of faces, but landscapes, lightning bugs, glass jars, and thunderstorms. After the rain gathered in its cracks, I sailed magnolia leaves down the driveway's isolated rivers. I searched for a pattern in the shallow runners of St. Augustine, each blade a whistle in waiting. And the carpet of moss under the cherry tree, droplets of dew perched at each stalk tip in which life grew itself— I wished myself small enough to crawl into that red bristled shag, walk the height of fronds in a forest of bracken.

All of this, as good as forgotten, as I moved in the certain flow of linear time, never asking: What will *let* itself be kept and what *wants* to fly away? We all might prove our human weight through measurement of human loss. When pushed, I looked and found a logic of dissolutions— a thousand tiny separations — and a child with her lens set out to magnify. I tried, I tried...

But I promise everything we've ever done seems to lead to some sort of sadness or loss, as nothing keeps its first flash for long, its slap and birth-cry, its firecracker pop, its lightning bolt snap that charges the air: not the rain pooling up, the spores of a fern dispersing, not the unfolded secrets that closed back up with daybreak's shifting streaks of fire and ice.

As highways have replaced the small rivers, mirages of heat shift like light on water and I'm floored by how much I don't know. But I *am* certain of one key thing: there's nothing more electric than the moment just after a secret has been told. Unless it is the odd familiarity of flowering quince lining the median, or the hum of tires on a freshly paved section of road.

2. The accidental rarefication of pattern #5609.

        This prosperity in our past went unrecognized.

We knew teacups   Noritake

to display in a proper

place.

            We cracked saucers.

       Each inadvertent drop

collected fame—

one teapot left   in a glass-front cabinet

from which we broke almost all the china—

they discontinued patterns   old styles

         which made the rules change:

common   to uncommon

available or scarce.

       We searched   wide—

the world's so indifferent to raising the dead.

3. I understand a little of my architecture.

It was a childhood.

There was a hammer to prick the wood with nails

and a plane to smooth the edges.

My father cut boards balanced across sawhorses,

rough wooden sawhorses – we made them manes and tails from rope

and I was the stable hand, catching sawdust in bowls

as it sifted down to feed them.

It was more than a game, my eyes drying in the powdered wood.

It was cool in the basement where the saws hung.

I'd bend the blades back and forth to make them sing.

The vice weighing down a corner of his workbench cranked open and squeezed closed;

its patinaed handle made my hands smell like blood.

***

The stain would spread and settle

into the ridges of my fingers.

We picked blackberries   along the roadside.

Brambles and snakes,   my arms scratched,

I thought of the boy in the schoolbook caught

in swarming bees and stung until he died.

It was summer for me, too,   and humid—

my legs stuck to the hot seat of the car.

I watched through the wide rear window

flanked by pails of black seedy fruit

as the road poured out underneath us.

We drove off into twilight,   the quiet

punctuated by dips of sonorous bats

chasing bugs

        through almost-dark.

***

The bridge stretched out for a mile over the bay.

Five hours in the car on the way to the beach

Seemed so much longer than the five hours home.

Sand crabs the size of my fingernails were pets,

Rotting in a green plastic bucket of sand.

Scratches on my legs from a fraying folding chair.

The sting of something in the water stirred up

By a storm. The crash of my father's voice inside

My head: *don't drop your fork on your plate!*

Pictures of me in the polka-dot bathing suit

With a funny-looking girl met in the water that day.

Pictures of the castle before the tide inched in

To its turrets built of a million tiny grains ground down

From shells and chitin by a turning, thrashing flood.

***

From the shade of the front porch swing I watched

my mother push her hands through dirt.

She taught me the names of bright things in our yard—

compact grape hyacinths, heavy scented magnolias,

blue jays that flashed and quarreled when we came too close to the nest.

She taught me tricks of forcing bulbs to sprout before they were ready,

taught me to weed the beds of chickweed and ground ivy and prune away

any undesirable traits, pluck aphids from swollen rose buds and hips.

I learned where poisons are found— in acuba leaves, mistletoe, foxglove—

while peonies bowed down to the ground

under the weight of petals and crawling ants.

Her marriage gone completely to seed, a season dry with no tears,

she raised me as an azalea when I wanted to be a green, fanning fern.

Some things were real,   others were not.

They worked away,   I chose my side.

In the end it was a table   and it was civilized.

4. The blue and white teacup was on the table—

and the ants that found the spilled sugar

also found the bowl of sunken fruit—

sweet, white lemons   given in to mold

with the oranges bruised around them.

Cups that broke.   Families that visited.

Socks slipped down   into shoes

         that stepped with forgetting.

     I lived there alone until a voice came:

     In the beginning you saw only one ant

walk the circumference   *of an orange*

but where you see one,   *you soon see more*

     and it begins to itch.

It's always this way when things start to crumble:

you've been disappearing   *for days now,*

like water seeping down a clogged drain,

or the way someone   eats that orange,

      a section at a time.

5. Every scrap of paper saved was sacred #1

In the certainty of fire— an echo—
of strong boots— black axes.

Philodendrons melt— like plastic—
plastic curls— like ribbon run along scissors—
half-eaten dresses— pile for the count.

Skeletons of box springs— curtains taken back to thread—

Mirror glass gone to shadow— windows turned to warnings—

Hear charred wood like a song stuck.

Speak of everything in terms of how it burns.

6. Calcination: Be careful— that's your grandmother's wedding china.

If you want to know what makes a face

it is the jaw and teeth:

when she fell and broke her hip it wasn't long

before I poked my nose over the coffin's edge.

we were the good undead, imitating her in a box,

pretending she was sleeping.

how real she looked: I stuck my index finger out

to touch her nose and cheek

and found they felt like wax.

this face, alive and resting, but not her face.

her false teeth rarely worn in life,

I saw how death disfigures.

this mouth, full of teeth,

and in her sudden jaw

***

Ox bones burned and crushed to dust,

mixed with mud and shaped to plates,

bowls take form in two thousand degrees

and cups will have saucers in which to rest—

to sit on tables, to sit on shelves,

to gather memories, gather dust

on the platinum trim, the scrolling lines

of grey and blue archaic leaves.

What did I want to be: record keeper or dreamer?

                                           I wanted some tea

and was handed a cup of red clay—

porous, unglazed,

wet— it sat in the small well of my hand.

An ounce of tea that went down hot,

left grit on my tongue and a smell of damp earth

against my face from this cup no one was meant to keep.

***

                  I learned of the heaps

of broken clay habitually tossed

against the tracks and lost

under the motion of trains and travelers' feet.

            I considered the future—   because this was not my life,

                                        and I could not let it go.

***

Is she cold or is she warm   *in her little cookie jar*

Take a teaspoonful and she   *will melt like sugar in your tea —*

Sand and ash, the sea is full   *of people burned and tossed*

Wooden spoons and Sunday best   *she is packed up with the rest—*

Metal fragments, bits of bone   *a recipe, a chance to atone*

Things crumble and fly away   *and you with your eye on yesterday—*

7. Every scrap of paper saved was sacred #2

(Burned it up, couldn't help myself— knew I could never keep it safe.

Ashes followed me around, I loved them like snow.

Why is it never cold enough here for magic?— water just goes down the drain, soaks into the sidewalk and the ground. Not like in arctic climates where water spurting from fire hoses freezes when it hits the air, hangs off street lamps, encases, drapes   what's left of the burned-out building:

a gothic ice cathedral, a glorious unintentional reframing of a mess.)

I am losing my music.

8. The Taxidermist

Pearl-ash.

Arsenical soap.

Corrosive sublimate.

    Do you know how to get blood out of feathers?
Press the eyes in but do not break them;
break the little bones between the orbits and the mouth.
Hoard. What you think you lack.
As a body retains water.
Be careful how you re-form the shell
once the fat is scraped away.
It can be either perched or poised for flight
but only one, then that forever.

        Here in the cracked house people come and go
more or less like anywhere else
but when something breaks it is often in slow motion.
We rewind, the chips and slivers recollecting
pulling into place to make of all things: a teacup,
and almost exactly the same one as before.
We are pleasantly surprised when the amber wave
sucks up into the shape of hot tea.
We also know the opposite is true:

a film of decomposition sped forward

appears to reanimate a dead thing—

the body of the little fox frantic with ants,

the saprobic swell of hydrogen and nitrogen,

that nods the head and wags the tail again.

This is a semi-permanent method

that does not require glue or wire.

                      But consider also a third option: it is

the animatronic pigeon's lack of a past that

makes him perfect. With only the pure drive

to move as intended and having nothing

he knows of to lose, he whistles open his wings,

mechanizes into the rafters. Such a beautiful sound

from under the mandible. The animatronic pigeon

is chewing his ambition into a whir and buzz,

singing for his supper of nuts and bolts.

9. Every scrap of paper saved was sacred #3

The fox's corpse animated with ants—
immaculate mechanical resurrection—
root systems spread out under concrete—
even in Chernobyl's wake—
the tv program says this will happen
when humans disappear from earth:
dogs will die trapped in our houses
where dishes stack still and soundless
till foundations shake and cabinets tip,
plates and cups crash to the floor;
buildings burn, but after that
clover sprouts from the blank charred fields.
In the forests of reclamation hang
half-buried hints of our once-existence—
your bicycle wheel woven into weeds—
the car you drove cross-country with
your father has bird nests under the hood—
old homestead sites of the Midwestern woods
reveal their former foundations by
clumps of daffodils and cracked stone steps

Look at the way we love the wreckage

each decade surfacing more of the lost

You can dig up what you planted, too—

have been thinking deep down in the soil,

Dead treasures buried in playground dirt

    you were the one who went away

the hand-drawn map inside your head.

climbing ghost feet into the air.

of that famous doomed ship,

with all our valiant new machines.

the bulbs you sunk away from sight

a tangle of roots to show for it.

accepted their funerals and stayed engraved—

yet was never lost,   *always seeing*

10. The White Phase

Bowls of sawdust and tufts of feathers—

dark peel of fruit and webbed wings of bats—

the ones who burn bones brush them into

a box but can they get every speck?

Soft but dense, the smoky must of age

is chalk on my tongue in this tannic bitter tea—

hard to swallow being left behind

but I would be scattered nowhere—

I would be glass made from sand

sintered in the furnace flames.

It happens in the body, happens in the brain—

memories break to chemicals in the end

resubmitting to ether for the start-again.

In that grave, a body treated with lime

gives off a blue-white light when it heats

as elements must have long ago

when burning to life in the cores of stars.

11. I changed the clock's expectations of me and
                    slept the extra hour hard and fast.

Why are you mad at time   when all it did

was wake you up?

                    Why are you blue

as a black eye,   putting on your shoes

two feet at a time?

                  There's nothing we can do

about the night.   It comes—

Reach.

           Each of us   receives a letter

from the Department Store that reads—

Dear Customer: *We regret to inform you*

your china pattern is no longer available.

You can sit and look at a blank white wall for hours.

You can stare off over the railing into the sea.

Go build yourself a world where bullets bounce.

If you were nearby you'd be singing.

We all live in other people's houses, fearing the spider electric.
A house is a body, network of nerves, arteries & bones.
Winter's a vast and friendless realm, in need of blankets and repair.

* * *

I come with a wrench for taps,
tap a tune of mending along pipes,
snake through ducts and feather insulation between beams.

* * *

Who am I making this nice for?
I'm half-charged, having curved too many smiles.

Mercury reverses:
in my mouth, a tongue and nothing right to say,
though the air is cold enough to catch the words.

* * *

Reaching for a door handle,
unfurling sheets   makes lightning—
branches of blue shocks.

Days go   I spark alone—
the nearest neighbors twenty yards away
and huddled behind black windows.

* * *

In this town of trees and subterfuge
built on stumps, watch the hands
around you— they use
trap doors, deadfall you in.

* * *

What is the sky doing now?
Is it black like those windows?
Planets stew in galactic soup—
infinity ladles our universe.

* * *

Cannot tell the difference between
the hands that want to steal me and
the ones that want to save me from myself.

* * *

I coast the long hill, worry my breaks.

A train hisses its approach in the cold metal of the tracks
long before it rumbles past me.

* * *

The moon does not rise and no one lives there.
It wears a blanket of cold rock all night.
Because it is cold, something on Earth is always in need of fixing.

* * *

I don't want to live under the moon's sway anymore.
I'm lost in endless rooms of my celestial house.

I'm abuzz with what isn't, with the requirements of distance—
oh put me on your shelf
and take me back down.

Loved Them Like Snow

In the days without music, light filled our quiet rooms.
Each day I woke in the sheer white of morning haze
and under winter's cover kept the hush
of photographs, neither joyful nor somber,
waiting to see if the weather would turn.

The best sounds were small and came from beneath
the silence that always accompanies snow.
We moved through the house,
unsure what we were listening for:

the sound of fly feet inside a taut lampshade,
the roots of amaryllis pushing through water and rocks,
filaments of mold boring into bread,
the ticking of reason within our bodies.

I slept beneath the spinning shadow of a mobile—
the planets and the untouchable Sun—
until the electricity went out, and my fingers turned so cold
they couldn't bend inside of gloves.
We dragged a mattress into the kitchen
and slept beside the gas stove until the ice melted.

But before that, in the room with the piano no one played,

my father had stood at the open door

staring into pink midnight

like he might hear a voice tell him what to do

but heard only the high limbs

of pines grown heavy with ice

cracking and shuddering to the ground.

Hunters

birds are falling through a Brueghel landscape
and there is no use in catching them
falling is the point

where did you leave your hair
where did you leave behind that other part
when did you give away the buttons on your coat
one for every *take off your shoes*
and stay awhile

now. what happens in these rooms
and outside of them
they'll cut that house to bits with bullets

behind black scrub brushes of trees
we fly on the ice
like birds on the ice

Ask Me

Out of the wind
away from the churn of tires
ask me how I got here
and why it was not some other place.

Ask me where I came from
an iron city, the Magic City, city of ghosts
from the blast furnaces, a haze overhead.

Here the air is more tender
I plant new seeds
some grow, others birds eat
the rent raises.

Ask me how I feel about reciprocity.

My roommate breaks up with her boyfriend
her child is still five
he watches television dressed like a ninja
there is an altar to romance in the fireplace.

Ask me what's next
into the water, into the worry, into the bed

something can happen now, and what will it be?

I'm not asking for you to answer
I'm not waiting
for a change in the weather or a
pattern in some leaves
I've already gathered all the signs I've seen.

Year of Dead Dogs

what did you do those days   the crow in the road was not a guide

when the bridge lay open to the other side   it was a scavenger

did you follow that big glassy crow   the sprung goldfish on the sidewalk

perched on the meter of a vacant parking space   was the wind under a fallen red leaf

           in the world of things not what they seem

did you listen to the man whispering   when you were buoyant

behind the mop-head hydrangeas   without a care

that drank up aluminum from acidic   umbels punched neon holes in the air but now that their blue's been drained

take the dried hydrangeas

to your father's house

tell him you had a bad dream

in which he looked too much like himself

    your secret vision skips a beat

soil under your bedroom window

there are shadows on the lawn

but this is not your house

the windows are too large

no steps lead up to your front door

Tell me spring is not

a wretched thing,

a Catherine wheel that wrecks

the air with bloom

I am hot, and can't sleep

I am mourning the passing

of sorrow

I am trying

to do it with grace

I am trying and failing

I went to the water

to escape

Sea air is Gemini air

Air near water

is mercury in action

Mercury is my drink

of choice

I did not swim out

looking for dark shapes

I stayed on the shore

A bird is a bird

I cannot fly

We were grounded

on the sand

in a useful way,

in the way that

roots are not always

something to fear

I've still got the grey sea

on my shoes

I've got a photograph

as proof of shadows

I'd like to say

I could take it

or leave it

but it sounds like summer

outside already

already golden

passing into green

I know your kind—

we would go on walks

at dusk through neighborhoods

scented with grass clippings

You would buy me

Coke Icees

I feel familiarity

which seems the

strongest emotion

But I do not

choose it

Two roads

in a yellow wood

and sorry, I—

looked down one I—

was clipped to the paths

of ideas and they undid me

I was forked

and following in my mind

thinking the man

who said it could

have gone down

both roads, just

one one day

and the other

the next

But every little thing

changes you—

you can't be

the same traveler, never

the same traveler twice

He watched

the trees shaking

off their clothes.

Please notice me!

they begged

Everyone I care about

is golden, everyone

I love is learning lines

and letting them fly

as a bird flies north

with the cosmos

in its claws

I am still

not a bird

and do not need to fly

down any other road.

The Flowerwaterers

> There are places and moments in which one is so completely alone that one sees the world entire.
>
> — Jules Renard

I did not find danger

in the middle of the night,

just men watering the baskets of petunias

that hang from tall street lamps.

I was an intruder in the secret workings

of a city, the washing of walkways

and store fronts, the chirp of garbage trucks

backing into their clanging cargo,

the hum of a gutter cleaner gliding along the grid,

all of them one step ahead, beating by only minutes the dawn

that would trade them for people with other destinations.

The Enigma of Arrival

> And what shall I love if not the enigma?
> — Giorgio de Chirico

Through the windows of the train car
Street lamps
The night snuck up
gradually into it
darkening earlier
wound down into coldness and rest.

the sky turned bluer.
came on a hazy pink.
and we moved
a part of this
as the season

When I was eight
did not revolve around me.
on a bright afternoon
to the landscape
The day had disappeared
like a boat cut loose from the shore,
like that shore after the boat is adrift.

I realized the world
Gone to the movies
we came back out to dark
transformed without our witness.
and night was in its place,

How many times since have I felt this same arrival into the significant moments of my life?

The Problem with Metaphysics

> Something is blotting out traffic.
> I hope it is the real night—
> the one that begins
> at the root of God's tongue
> and breaks in my mouth
> and tastes like ink.
>
> — Bill Bogart

On the night the past catches up with you

it's impossible to not fall in love

with what you know so distinctly you cannot have.

On the night you say too much,

the air turns golden with captivity,

and all the unkept promises run

like mice through the attic of your head.

This is the movie of your life.

When the theme music finds you,

let it follow you down the street

as you walk that solitary pace,

clutching your dance card in your fist.

Up the hill past the red eyes of the empty church,

past the apartment where a friend once lived,

you recite the night in your head and also out loud

because you have no pen to write it down,

the sound of your own name ringing oddly wrong in your ears.

You wish the man walking towards you could

lift you into his breast pocket with all his loose change,

but he just tips his baseball cap without a word

in an underrated gesture, long lost and forgotten,

reminding you of the negative spaces of your life.

You recall how the sun repositioned itself throughout the day

and how much you have always

hated the smell of daisies; you recall a promise

that came in the mail: hundreds of dollars

in tax relief money, returning from the abstract world.

In this life, they sell notions at the corner store,

vague as smoke or specific as a button.

Take what you can get, like the jar of marionberry jam

the previous tenant left in the refrigerator,

even if the seeds will stick in your teeth.

You keep walking, trying to remember what you used to do

on Thursday nights, what you used to say,

in this neighborhood that tonight smells electrical.

Nothing is what it seems; even the sliver

of light above the trees that you thought was the moon

is only a faulty street lamp pulsing before the black sky.

How loud your shoes sound against the pavement.

Mystery and Melancholy of a Street

Every day the city expands by tearing down.
>The wrecking ball's ten thousand pounds
slam and powder history until no one
>can remember what used to be:
this street of shadows rolled to the horizon,
>the open carriage of birth called you back,
the specter of a man loomed
>and promised around the corner.
How good it felt to be wanted,
>almost saint-like, almost holy
against a backdrop of antiquity
>your primeval sense of having
belonged somewhere specific,
>to have inhabited.
Among scores of broken tile
>and splintered wood composed
by the claw of the backhoe,
>you feel as hollow as a hoop.
When glass crumbles
>into brick, it doesn't matter
what was done out of fairness
>and what was done out of spite;
someone is spilling secrets into the air.

      In the shell of a building,
pigeons lift, fill the rafters
      with a bad and persistent silence.

Explanations / Excuses

after Giorgio de Chirico, *Turin Spring*, 1914

Because the hand is perpetually heavy

because the flower is full of string

because the horse is frozen in cantor

because of architecture and because of stars

because you never opened the book

because the earth only spins so far each day

because where the day takes you may not be where you wanted to go

because all men are potential fathers

because we think we are wired for love

because there is a difference between yes and yes

because the flag waves in surrender

because redemption only comes to those who ask

The Unfair Hours

Life's not fair, my mother always said,

it never having occurred to her to fight for what she wanted.

I was raised to love the sacrifice

and never mind the blame.

But I know her silent life was something else—

Sundays, she'd drive alone down the highway out of town

when it was a strip cut straight

through rock face and hardwood.

She could've kept on going had she dared.

Here, the streetcars loop on infinity,

returning me unscuffed to the same house—

one story white, black shutters— where

the geraniums on the porch are red as ever.

Almost nothing's changed,

though a few petunias may have folded for the night.

How different my life might have been

if my mother had instead been able to say:

Here. Take this.

Learn to make it your own.

I might have been anything,

but now I am this

and every time is like the first,

coming home to fire,

to the smell of burnt toast.

Still, I find there is no need to beg.

Nasturtiums

> I would rather show you the nothing in my sky-blue eyes than give you an answer about it.
>
> — Hans Arp

Little brains burst open in the soggy soil

underneath the mulch of last year's vines.

Seeds, please come back and be

your old selves, have something inside.

Some grow robust, some spindly,

reaching for a sun that doesn't shine

or if they sprout somehow

too late in the season

scorch, dry up, in the heat.

They wanted to be, and tried,

but every drop of water given

opened more stomata and they lost

that water to the unforgivable air.

*

Love burns up the Knight of Cups' essence.

Evaporates itself with need. To you

everyone is sacred. This trips

all my alarms. Hierarchy

pleases me, I need to reign

atop the tallest sunflower in the field.
I need differentiation— let the hollow seeds
float to the top and save the viable ones,
the ones with potential to feed.

*

Life, you sad fuck, always losing your footing.
Empty chairs, filled coffins, flowers sent too late.
People in restaurants talking to each other.
People in restaurants not talking.
I am jealous of still lifes
even though their impossible arrays
are descriptors of everyone's deaths.

*

When we have
a lot,
we use a lot.
When we are
running low
we know
how to manage
with the littlest
possible.
The famous great man
on my t-shirt

has died

and I'm standing

over the stove

making box mac

& cheese, heating

this can of peas that

Nostalgia says to eat.

A few good lines

promise to be more.

A flood of acceptable grief.

*

You grieve alone.

It scares me.

I'm scared.

I'm scared of dry days.

I'm scared of too much rain.

I'm scared of our fathers dying,

the tailspin that will be.

When I have not heard your arguments,

when I have not seen your misery,

I picture you like a Schiele self-portrait,

skin sinking under bones.

Your dirty orange robe

is the color of nasturtiums.

You cover one eye

and then the other

trying to move objects
around the room.
Terror wants to erase you,
uproot the screaming seed.

*

Babies cry in public
and it bothers me.
Babies cry,
it's their nature,
but on this night
everything
must be investigated.
Static from the tv
enters dreams.
Disappointment
eats away at love.

*

You don't grieve alone. You call me, you come here. We lay on the bed, half on/half off. Death makes us tired. I fall asleep with your cock in my hand, unable to do anything about it. From now on we might be one bit less interesting to each other, though you've been hoarding your past so we'll have something to talk about in the long future we vaguely plan.

*

You mean to be true but things sneak up.

You black out, get home

but can't remember how.

There are songs to make a case

for what is to your left, or your right,

or across from you.

The one with the car keys and the car.

A room nearby.

Would be me were I invited.

It starts in coffee shops.

In-between-times trump scheduled times.

You live in the Aether.

Where are your hands?

You cannot actually leave

them here.

*

What if resurrection

were the actual inevitable?

Is to say *I loved* to say I no longer love?

It is not— I did, I still do, I have throughout.

But the phrasing— the phrasing matters.

*

I would wave a magic wand, close the book of my life a little, dim the light of the moon so no one could see me measuring. Open book, open book— too much sparkle, not enough. Love does all the things the moon does, but the moon does it better. I slide the beads of an abacus up and down not understanding how this is math. My fingers smell of brass. I resort to clichés but try to bend them back to the visual.

*

I want to be a fly on the wall

I want to be the ghost in the machine

I want the Halo God of Dark Things

to slide the velvet down

I want to put souls into objects

I want the testimonial of houses

still standing under oaks

I want now and not after-the-fact

I want a sunrise and a sunset in the same day

I want coffee twice, and breakfast made at home

I want to keep the weeds at bay with dinner reservations

I want hotels in other places

I want to *be* my shadow, and bend around corners

I want grasshopper legs

I want a feathery instinct

I want a paper valentine

I want infinite chances

I want a little sugar for my hysteria

I want to carry your misery in my teeth

I want the reliability of chemicals

I want the sigils to burn and work

I want to wear your shirt

*

Book of my life, already written—

book of your life, written in mine.

High bridge out my window, thick pink end-of-winter air.

Car lights shine through it, flying, like flying, like they'd meet me

in the inevitable space inside vision.

We need the salt and the silence but also the miracle.

Soon it will be time to plant again. Soon, not yet.

Apples rot in the bowl but they are not mine.

Fruit flies accept the challenge of a momentary false spring.

Nothing at All or Everything at Once

a salvation of objects
shelves and cabinets full
a room full of ghosts with fingers
maybe it's a butterfly
maybe it's a twist of fibers
a signature, a watermark
outside a schoolroom window
sparking in the sun

my tellurian self   still
ley lines severed
a day is undercut by the menace
the grit of your affection
too quiet for higher ears
I had already made up my mind
I should feel free but
warm the blood of the hands
these interior changes give rise
I remember magic

a suffocation of objects
and full of dust
tangled in their hair
or maybe it's a bird
left over from last year
a pool of rain on the roof
a bath for goldfinches
twenty golden boats
my first aetheric vision
a memory almost aged out

a no-man's land
instead of walked
of not knowing how to spend it
insect hum of insect teeth
kills off a little bit more
I just hadn't told you yet
I come away snarling
by slapping them together
to a magical worldview
turn into a bird to escape

Counting Across a Finite Field

In the world of sea monkeys, each undulation makes a wave.

Do not peek at caterpillars returned
in pupae to primordial ooze
or you will ruin the angels.
Let earthworms hacked regenerate
in damp and dark of peat—
things *want* to live.
Ferns catapult their spores
into an afternoon's hot haze
and hope to flare an army of
green arrows across the dirt.
I watch bits of lace frill and grow
inside this glass on my desk
and know I have seen the true face
of *the small*, magnified and natural
with appetite. Everything minute moves
swiftly to its orchestrated place,
a fitting form to realize every goal.
I think of beds in rooms, tightly made
and how I am made and unmade much like those
as others lie down in me and change my shape.

Before It Was This

I'm interested in how wintergreen burns and how it sparks—

    into dark closets or bathrooms with the lights shut off

    the girl lured the boy to prove with teeth

    the green electricity hidden inside of Lifesavers.

    I'm interested in bioluminescence and the arcs of comets.

    Launched in permanent paths, they drag debris

    in gaseous tails across the universe and most

    will never come back around before you die.

I'm interested in permanence, what room could hold me.

    Out of what window do I want to see all mornings?

    Are the rotating views of seasons enough?

    Will I keep using this same cup to drink my coffee

    and what will I do if it breaks?

I'm interested in how we make each other more.

    The cup you chose is metal.

    Since it can't break, you must not be afraid

    to drink from something that will outlast you.

I'm interested in the clever ocean wiping the slate clean.

    A gull stands atop a dune of sparking sand,

    shifting from foot to foot.

        Hours are fences.

Flowers, uninterested, shut down for the night.

        I can't tell you what to do.

        I turn in my sleep.

        Sound enters the dream and becomes a body.

I Only Wanted You for Your Warmth

    after Kandinsky, Untitled, 1941

that's us	a bloodmetal tang
blown to oblivion	lemon juice
inside the shark's mouth	in the wound
cold comfort	our table, our Tower
in the water	flies square off
red oaks	in the middle of the living room
Mother's Day	will not give up
confetti, a parade	the pattern
a light-up dance floor	I know you are
pulsing a decade of birthdays	but what am I
splash of a fountain, pink & blue	by the time
against the city sparkle overlook	I messaged you
placesetting poised	we had already lost
in napkin swans, radish roses	Idontknow
carrot nests, apple doves	how, still
worm in the apple spoils	our borders run
the geometry of the cut	nearly
scissors & saws	to the edge

The Tilting Horizon Over the World Full of Holes

after Brueghel's Landscape with the Fall of Icarus

1. Is Pretending to Fly the Same as Flying?

Who could say how it felt   that close to the Sun   it melts fibers
that bind ideas   gods played with the shifting   textures of the world
bodies part felt, part clay, part bone   an orchard of candles
on your back   ground left behind   your father, a thief
who left you in the sea   ill-equipped   to fish you out
grief is a labyrinth   even if the Minotaur is dead.

2. Navigating the Maze

I was aware of Mercury's tilt and turn, aware of the movement backward that, in fact, wasn't movement at all but an illusion. It had just gone direct, in fact, when my birthday returned in the year 2015, and on that same day in June, a meteor named Icarus was passing very close to the Earth, so close, in fact, that five decades before, scientists had made a plan to knock it out of the sky but then, for some reason, decided not to. Perhaps the irony was too much for them; they were afraid to act as that great hot Sun. Once was enough for the child to suffer, even as a namesake only. But back to that birthday— on that birthday I was, in fact, not celebrating. I was, in fact, losing the job that was my Sun. I was losing it but also I was letting it go, allowing the heat to melt the wax I thought was holding my wings together. That was not, in fact, the case. In fact, as the barometer confirmed, it was fear of empty space, the wax sealing every hole, that weighed me down.

3. Crossing the Threshold

For Nature abhors a vacuum. For The Fear of Empty Space is a real and serious thing. For there is tremendous pressure at the edge of a void. For this is The First Rule of the Game: respect your boundaries. *For one would define void as place bereft of body,** but what is *body*, is air a thing? *For when the water* [body] *and the air change places, all the portions of the two together will play the same part in the whole which was previously played by all the water in the vessel.** For if Place is a vessel that cannot move, then my body, also a vessel filled to its borders, must be the thing to move. For if my body is to be in The Place where you are that cannot move, something else must be displaced within those walls. For maybe air is all you need. For there is no void.

* Aristotle, *Physics*

The Path & the Obstacle

1.

I had said I wanted a real snow and then it came down
fast and thick, made the trees look like spring,
the ground feel like sand, like walking through dunes.
It does not matter to me if the trees bloom;
that is a byproduct in its beauty
of this preferred landscape.

2.

I said I wanted it to stay, to stop time
so I could hide out,

said I wanted to play in the Otherworld that had been conjured in ice,
leave my mark in deep rivets of footfalls along the road.

3.

Said I wanted to take my home with me

when I went places in the world.

I build a virtual world. Yours is the only like I look for.

I find a consistency of brutal opinions.

I find an inconsistency of honest attention.

I find enemies and disappearances.

4.
In one fairytale, the queen has no joy.
The jesters craft a play for her
and the king laughs along.
He glances aside to share the moment,
but finds her ashen and pinched.
Someone has taken her joy.
These clowns cannot replace it.
The man in black makes her a deal
but such deals require a death in exchange.
Whose death is never specified
at the time the bargain is struck.

5.
The Game of Self is played constantly.
You can play mine;
I'm writing rules in the air all the time.
When the rules change, you will know
because the weather will correspond.

6.
What *do* you like?
Where are you going?
Who will be there?

And how will you get home?

7.

There have been other queens who liked to carve their kingdoms out in ice.
They are never written about kindly. They stick icicles in hearts
and call it love.

8.

I practice such obliteration.
I scratch up my path like a chicken so no one can follow.
Bury it under a foot of lace.
Make myself impossible.
I cast you out. I cast myself out.
Take the first available ghost and plant it inside.

9.

The crackle of a dead record—
a record's end—
is the sound of a brushfire, spreading.

What occupies us so
we can't restart the needle?

10.

The news clip I don't want to see
plays in the corner of the screen.
Clicking to shut it up only makes it bigger.
Opinions are even louder

against the hush of snow outside.

11.

I am afraid of the news, big and small.

Afraid of the black box, the screen.

Afraid of print, of being seen.

12.

We live in the shadow of the castle we have made.

Would you come for me if the Tower crumbled?

Not everything worth doing can be done at a distance.

13.

The course of a fever includes the chills.

Once you learn this, you never forget,

but in the moment the coldness feels unending.

Penance

after Aubrey Beardsley's *Salome with the Head of John the Baptist,* 1893

The world is a box

of annoyances   (you said).

I've willingly given my share.   (Been loud for months.

              Time to be quiet. Be clean. Submerse.)

    A world of haze and halting—

    A world of shovels to bury—

The pretty little puffs on those branches are made to fall off

                      even if you don't touch them.

        A kiss at a bus stop   (mine for you)—

           An ogre of affection   (no bus came)—

      A threshold of fog   to walk through

    which churned on, in veils,

        and me out—

                      (No, don't dance!)

all axes—

on one side, someone loved—

un-witch me

(what you did with that fruit)—

it never stops raining now,

ribbons,

in the gutters,

city flooding

(Go under!)

the flowers are thriving—

No! Don't unhitch me—

I went too far—

Would you like a glass of water

before you sleep—

fitful,

you would sleep

better next to me

underneath the round

black clouds

and all this water,

the sky unhinging.

It is not water—

the room is filling with it fast—

What am I not giving you that you need?

The flattened squirrel every day for a week
wicking away under wheels spinning in.

Map a new route on thin tires.
Carry the old dog up and down stairs
at least six times each day.

The way he tells me
he would like more water
is to lick
                                      the inside of the empty bowl until I fill it.

We must be more careful.

Life is a fist of roots   in part
but what grows above the surface gets easily mowed.

When we do die
we'll get to choose
the age we want to be forever
and which pet,
but only one.

It Takes Me by Surprise

To kiss the cloud was tough as it swung its slag and fisted rocks in my face.

I wanted to garden, to stake my claim, but it curved the blue, wavering sky

away from any fruitful place until the drive was washed away. The mud

it makes says nothing works, nothing stays and nothing rights. Nothing

in the eyes I use—　　　　they're faulty

in their hot decay of memories shaping red dismay and fear of strangers

turning close. I am a dog for soft attention breaking

in the held-over dawn, one hand on midnight's disappearing walls

and one on now's shy hope. The chance that it will fall apart

is bruised about my throat.

The Light and the Clouds Came In

Time clicking on,

a lyric, a din

in the bells of the church,

the anticipated toll.

Same cup, same companion,

assumptions of home.

We sit over cereal

and play our

dumb roles.

Rilke's lines punish me

I know I am seen—

the room of blurred light swallows

me whole

in an idea of exit,

elixir of brightness,

carriage to a place

where nothing is owed.

A crunch in each knuckle

and not friends at all—

these hands could be scissors

or swans or oars.

It's Sunday again

one minute till nine.

Nothing here to hear

but the sound of spoons in bowls.

St. Clare rifles through a pile of receipts.

I'm dead you know,

        lost my *fascinating*.

        Crawl in a hole,

be able to stay down?

Look at that window again…

        full of dark morning.

The ghost who sits on my chest at night.

The time it takes to count lightning distance.

                When I leaned in closer

that man was without scent.

        Feel a little funny;

        I will try to make a list.

St. Clare is nourished by the mere elements.

        Winter   and everywhere.

Lost gloves on sidewalks.

Ghosts of fingers.

                Emptied but for air.

In books they weave permissions back and forth.

A long dash belongs to sequestered women.

(Ordered one more

excuse to stay   )

        A long dash—   a pause.

        A long dash—   a request.

        An implication.

A reach.	A branch of palm placed in my hand.

	I am your nun.

St. Clare takes her Orders.

       You are my strange twin— no way else to say it.

I've oversaturated you?   Might you dry out again like a sponge.

       Then I accept.

What unshared we have done

in thought of each other—

constant thinking is as good as letters

not delivered, pages winded   across a green field.

       Does it shift

              in your mind

                    as in mine?

St. Clare talks to The Cross.

Voice like a mouse   or a radiant angel?

                              What would you expect—

            Wasn't a voice at all   really.

            Hands on smooth stone.   Palm fit to a warm groove.
            A vibration offered:

                  Give   to the intangible

              what was already given to the intangible man.

St. Clare does the laundry, folds the sheets like flags.

My life was small but I've made a country of it.

        Owning nothing

        is open enough to get lost.

I was a girl beneath your scissors:

your hands in my hair, my hair in piles.

Now, ground sleeps hard.

Days without talking.

Fabric creases quietly.

Confession wells.

St. Clare cleans the house for company.

      A message of your arrival arrives on a dove—

                I sweep out all the corners.

Potential burns my mouth   in prayer.

Are you coming to find what I am now?

I sneak up on an idea

that I'm a vessel   but for what.

You look the same—

    I show you

    your incorruptible self.

    I'll keep us safe—

    all green , no blush.

                The rooms immaculate,

                clutter shoved out of sight.

St. Clare admits: *Our bodies are not made of brass.*

        But also not made for each other?

You already married Poverty.

        She's prettier than me.

But your hands   for all their small castings under Heaven's broad eye

are still hands.   Mine flex and twitch—

            the weight of your palm

            your rough, ridged fingertips

            chip-nailed

            un-mine.

St. Clare questions the tether of spirit to relic.

You run as a current within me

how   how can we be

    separate.

I can smell the metal in you, I can hear your doubt—

    though blind

        you preach to the birds.

Then your hands are gone,

    gone instruments of industry and grace.

    Gone you,   all borders erased.

    For me   this earth, a great cage.

    Someone else's book of stories

        in which I carry on

        as me, as you.

        Astonished Angels watch up on our Cross—

        their mouths form little o's of anticipation   .

Life

Baseball caps

Silly putty

People I have loved

People with real careers

Hot tea gone too cold to drink

Layoffs and leavings

A better way to think

Gum resting on the roof of my mouth

Something I can't remember

My garish face, sometimes

Sun lifting the color out

The lean-in

The dodge

We are the displacers of what happened before

Titles are the first to go

Erased from a prayer

The furnace coughing out old smoke

Names are next

Faces widening

The skull of the moon

A great connector who never connects

Falling asleep in the middle of it

Every time we don't

A scorpion in the shoe

A safe full of fears

People I've wronged

People who've wronged me

The liars and the cheats

Silly little girls with silly little crushes

Vultures suck the air out with their wings

Tell me you'll never

Pretend I didn't

Try to like music again

This place where we sleep

Where we wish we slept

A phone charging on the bedside table

A phone charging across the room

A phone on silent

One missed call

A midnight run

Fear deep in the gut

Extinction as a form of flying away

If you can't see it, it lives forever

Existing on a plane within the other plane

When I was a little girl I saw the future

Was lost in it, looked up

And saw the Great Brain at work above

Everything under the sun can be ours if we ask

We have been steadily climbing our way up

When there is no cat, we can do what we want

The way children must chase rabbits

Feel the soft fur against their cheeks

Congestion speaks as a ringing in the ears

Makes a room of one's own

I will make a singular music

A blade of grass in the gap between joined thumbs

Found in a field – a song

Life is an object

Wasn't it always just this way?

Hearing you while I also hear myself

No, no, I don't think so

Lift the veil of my delusions

A Sudden Swerve

It became available, this truth,
that innocuous things could swarm at any moment.
You and the world retreated, though not together.
Were the budding branches of plum trees still
the long cold arms of winter? In the sudden snow,
they snapped, and the edges of what you'd called
"essential solitude" were frayed like the splintered
ends of those limbs and impossible to root.
You returned to your faraway house,
even with the sky so unpredictable,
and even with the facts of mystery confirmed
by mysterious alignment of our tangible twin worlds.
Below every surface is a well of feeling.
You moved your body carefully along the meniscus,
braced for the next acquisition
after the fallout, after the swarm
settled back down,
cloaked itself again in the everyday.

Feathers and Lead

I Am Nothing's Mother

Every night I fold the world up
and every morning   I open it again.
There are days for talking and days for hands.
Days for planning and days for teeth.
There are days to sit and watch the shadows of bees
dart past the windows in the garden.
I think of the brightness that gives them grey ghosts,
that copies them onto any surface.
They think of hives and are far from home.
The way I feel about myself is because of the light.
It angles onto a face favorably or it slants
along the jaw and nose revealing the beast.
Should I hide from my father, the Sun,
become a pale lettuce, bitter at the core?
What is a root   deep and wide beneath   but a shadow-self?
Should I be the black shadow over all the insects of the garden?
In the angle without light, I carve myself   out of myself,
I carve myself out of space, carve a self-sized space in the air,
become the air, become the stretch of shadow.
From here I can cast my aethereal line
and I can lengthen my gaze like an antenna
to the depths, to the depths, to the depths,   to deaths,
to the dealing   the undoing   the retrieval.
Because I looked at the Sun so long,
its opposite is clear when I close my eyes.
If I am not a being of the Sun,
am I of the Moon the satellite, the mother,
that hovers over fear of emptiness?

The Earth considers itself in revolutions,
a double-agent to dual spheres.
Bees plan the path home, always the same path,
but a year becomes shorter every year.

Seven Days

In the beginning there was a cart and no horse,

nowhere to go beyond the cul-de-sac, the creek bed and the cave.

I curated   a legacy of dishes   tutored by the Mother of Worries.

Relatives were frequently sick and needing to go to hospitals.

They would be taped back together   and we would go back home and keep on living.

Their kitchen counters served pill bottles by days of the week.

I suffered through allergy shots so I could go outside

then Blistex for chapped lips in winter at bedtime.   She said

the burn means it's working. She said that for Bactine, too, on skinned knees. I craved the smell.

We outlasted the Hospital People;   one by one went under itchy grass.

Today, tomorrow, but not forever   is the meaning of the pillbox now on my nightstand.

You might think using it would encourage the wrinkles, but I see it as a gift of foresight:

I'm certain I'll make it the next seven days.

I feel good that each one   has something of the same in it—

a smaller cart   with just enough horsepower.

That breeds philosophy   as much as epiphany does.

Not to adhere, not to worship,

I practice my philosophy like a craft,   to get good at it.

That's why I'm a light sleeper.

I hear little feet thumping down the hall,   water turning on and off,

the house stretching,   the moon counting down.

Things happen at night.

The teenage boyfriend   who dumped the teenage me for being too sad years later fell off a mountain   in Africa and died.

They said it was nighttime,   that he lost his footing.

He only had a dark horse, too eager to gallop.

My life had been a constant museum.

I had to grow up sometime.

Beyond the material crust float rough rocks we've named.

I bet they call themselves something else   or nothing at all.

Immortal horses trample the firmament, dragging a golden chariot behind.

I still believe in Pluto's authority, the key and scepter,

believe the sky is the son of Aether and the Earth.

It rains here, then it doesn't,   yet we trust the weather report.

There may be a 100% chance of rain,   but what kind of rain and how much, for how long?

When it's time to change, change.   Bring the leaves down in waves, make a hole where no hole was before. Drown the starter self in shallow mud,

no cart, no horse, just a pattern of seven days gradually loosening

until there is only one, but it's the only one you need.

The Cinnabar Fields

Found afield, a blade of grass

singing in the gap

between joined thumbs.

*

We have ideas

and we are burning

to project them.

*

We have ideas and they are burning us up.

*

Magician stones are cinnabar

and cherry red garnets.

Standing inside a ring of fire is Process.

Fire is a mood and an antique tool.

*

Time is on fire and disappearing into blackened wisps,

into embers that scratch apart in the grate.

*

The mechanical fortune teller

has confirmed this for fifty

years in the same slow

jerking movements.

*

The increasing gentleness of adulthood
weighs on some in a progression of Wednesdays;
for them, to douse is to capture.

*

I do not think the Alchemists tired of turning lead into gold.

*

The Magician cuts wands
on Wednesday, Woden's Day,
the day of Mercury.

*

Mercury sulfide of the red-spotted stone
held in a salty palm
activates the Trinity.

*

There is no fire without air.

*

The whistle in the grass.

Who will not run?

> ...its general appearance can best be expressed as being like an umbrella pine, for it rose to a great height on a sort of trunk and then split off into branches...
>
> — Pliny the Younger, *Selected Letters of Pliny*

The volcano at the Science Fair actually worked
and spewed its baking soda foam
down the paper mountainside.
Chemical reaction, it bubbled and rushed the rough
slope toward the tiny Pompeii's cobbled streets,
Play-doh villas, shrubs, even a bakery.

Missing here, as Pliny described it,
the ash that moved like a flood on land,
the sky that broke into a red-hot pumiced rain
until there was no daylight in the day—
absolute black of a windowless room
in which families   searched for each other
by their voices   in the dark.

The actual deaths— so very quick—mid-action in the pyroclastic heat—
one moment reaching for a door—the next forever in that reach—

*He hurried to the place which
everyone else was hastily leaving,*
the Younger said of his uncle, the Older,
who stood on the shore to see it better
before the fumes choked and felled him like a tree,

    proof that there are some who will not run,

    who want to see it coming for them—

    to look up into the stars until

    smoke and ash   or their failing eyes

    blot out every   last one.

Museum of Glass & Bone

> If you have a choice between two things and can't decide, take both.
> — Gregory Corso

1. City of Rain, Sidewalks of Glass

Science happens most when we look away,

with shifts too slow to detect

with day-to-day patience:

when light breaks, a loaf of bread sits dry,

bag twisted tight. Today we leave home

in favor of a world of infinite choice:

a well-lit café in our city of glass

and exactness of orders that always come with toast.

First the morning, then the day,

then the night comes, brings the rain.

Behind the orange juice, marmalade crystallizes,

forming tiny nuclei and growing glass in rings,

the bread bag already a house for spores—

hyaline hyphae bore into pores

and the forgotten loaf blooms.

2. Under a Microscope

Like trees in winter, iced over,

the halted sap hibernating inside.

Like human hair in front of light.

Like floaters that sling across my eyes

and flip like hydra in a drop of pond.

Hyphae, tiny tubes of glass,

conidia in loops and chains,

rhizopus towers, aspergillus flowers—

spores small enough to fit

through the eye of a needle,

thin as memories can,

crystalline threads fusing

and snapping with age.

3. Before

Four boys circled it, the robin at the edge of the playground, its heart ripped out by a cat's sharp mischief. They poked it with a stick, probed the hollows of bones brittle as glass. That heart, a foot from its chest, in the middle of boys— flip a coin, draw straws— someone had to pick it up to know what it weighed, to learn its texture, while the rest watched. It was a pivotal moment, staging for the person each would later become when put to the test.

4. And After

(The whole of the bird and inside the bird.
Heart.Eggs.Bones.
& all the parts that aid in flight.
Use them enough and they lose known values
the way glass melted down pools for a new shape,
the way bread becomes a feeding forest,
the way we no longer reflect for each other
the selves we like best.)

5. Liquid or Solid?

> And glass… is so much like water.
> — Dale Chihuly

In the Hot Shop everything is moving,
but in the Cold Shop a surface
exists to be etched.

I tried to ask
but I guess it's not so simple.

Over the river, a bridge of glass,
tall towers of candyglass, flat sheets
of moving water. Water
freezes, glass melts.

If what seems solid is not
how would architecture change?

Could you walk on water,
could you swim through glass,
could cracked windows heal themselves
or would they never break?

6.

What I said before about exactness isn't true.
At restaurants I never get what I order.

When I was little my father was
the kind of man who sent things back,
so I am the kind of woman who cries
over sour milk, scrambled instead
of poached, rye rather than whole wheat.

7.

In a *hand-blown glass bell*
the spondees ring.

When the dying woman

comes briefly back
she tells us: *There were trees.*
She says nothing else all day
and keeps her eyes closed.

8.

In the dark and in the cold
handle me like glass.
Blow into my brittle hollow so that I can fly.

When we said we would always
have breakfast together
we couldn't imagine wanting
anything else.

So much preparation goes into disappointment:
we try, we twist the tie,
we push and twist the air out of the bag.
We bundle up, fasten each loop
around the buttons on our coats
although we know the air is getting in—

Strive, try again—
another window, another way
to move the sap through the hollows,
to perfect your ordering or to love what you receive,

what grows on the surface or beneath,

until some future morning when
our glass houses on their long thin poles
rise up over the fog.

Monsters

    I'm always in my boat

                                                                   trying to carry a message to
                                land.

                    set with its semaphore sails

    I sail the air

                                                  The madness of clouds

              but don't know where I'm going.

    makes me push on—

                                                under a fat-faced sun.

                  giant tongues of cirrus lick the sky

    I'm not sure why my sail is sucked back like a body in a syruped dream
    with limbs   that won't   move forward—

    I'm not sure why the air is soaked in the sweet revolve of memory.

    I've been unfair   thinking I'm not lost too.

    But my hair swells   with salt and wind.
    Bet you didn't know   how it naturally wants to curl—

* * *

The night is an island   within an island
accessed by a narrow   gap we must steer through.
The Moon is just   a comma in space—
I know you use it   that way too,
wish the roots would   plant down more
reach the center of   the night and hold it in place.

But the Sun is risen   on both sides.

How do we sleep when   there is so much to do
that can't be done off   our dark island?

I've been trying to tell you a story now for days.

Cannot Be Sustained

Because my fear is an animal in its own right it gnaws at bindings.

Because you might prefer many to one, or zero to any, no more pictures were requested.

Love is not natural; it is a dazzling threat that asks an excess of questions.

What are you up to… what card did you pull today… do I still come talk to you

in your actual dreams? I did not knowingly penetrate the borders of your consciousness

though I would like to have gotten in there, endosymbiotically, in the way that

chloroplasts are primary endosymbionts of plants, providing energy by generating sugars,

or the way that *Oophila amblystomatis* grows exclusively on the eggs of the spotted salamander.

Are we afraid of being enveloped, consumed? What is freedom?

Everything changes. In the movie we each watch a second time,

deer sprout flowered antlers. Throats rip open

to let new things grow inside, but first there is resistance, suspicion of motives. No one is being honest.

My glowing cells spark like neon suns, divide in so many twos.

By the time you get here, I will have become someone else, altered by divisions and by visions, the secret world I found beneath crystal trees. Tell me soon, before I start running.

Tell me before I cross the field and turn into a tree.

Everything Is Red

after Mark Rothko

Carnations, carnelian, heartaches and blush

Cardinals, some apples, the Sweetgum in fall

Cap gun tips and cowboy hats, a squealing afternoon

Birmingham dirt, fire ant mound, the swarm spilling into my shoes

A dodgeball war, the welts like lace

Every other zinnia flower, the Chinese Garden gates

Cut bloodroot, cinnabar rings

Wax around a wheel of cheese

Turkish rugs, highway lines,

A. muscaria under the pines

The rooster's head, the kitchen walls

The devil and everything growing tall

The phone call

The clock dial

The cause and explanation

The sorrow, the red sorrow

Words spelled wrong on screen

My hands full of splinters, your hands full of blood

The cushion you knelt on to reach me where I stood

When the night dropped its black, observant hush

The red light of dawn made a play on the wall

Couldn't Say, and Didn't: Part 1

> …like having fangs is something to regret,
> like we shouldn't give thanks for blood
> thirst…
>
> — Dean Young, "Could Have Danced All Night"

Problem is, I'm against migration.

Problem is, I can't like anything that doesn't like me back.
This goes for objects too, and places.
How they can show it.

Oh well. Look @ your pretty pictures. Stranger.   I met you again
                                     and again nothing happened.

I won't travel for cornfield jobs or skyscrapers unless this place is ruined by a
specific vacancy and I have to kill off the image of *that* city in my mind.

What loves me back with paved roads
and sometimes sea air and proper saloons
I know doesn't really, but it lets the food I grow use its dirt.

I try to see myself as a machine. Crank on.

Couldn't Say, and Didn't: Part 2

Go to the door and unlock it.
Go to the door and don't knock.
Go to the door and find me inside when you open it.
Standing like a statue when you open it.

Come apart in my hands.

When you were lying dead on the beach it was only a dream.

When you dissed me in the movie theater it was only a dream.

If you would just let me let me let me let me let me—

Some things only happen once. Be careful or you'll miss them.

Couldn't Say, and Didn't: Part 3

When to the heat

I commit my skin

I cannot rise too fast.

That woman I hate is still alive
though one day she won't be.
That ruining woman is still alive inside.
Outside, she lives in a house near mine,
an uncomfortable distance for a nemesis.

Things waiting to bite have simple names so you may not see them coming.
Should I be punished for bringing them into the house on my hair?

Must do away with everyone who calls me by the old name.

People I know are always there in the room,

and so am I, but also never.

Couldn't Say, and Didn't: Part 4

Cold stone to warm-blooded.

Coarse salt to well-spoken.

A Little Princess, dethroned by the shore,

couldn't learn to like

the kind of life she could afford.

Whether or not she understood

the allure of legs, she got them,

and wobbled through her compromise,

duped speechless. But like a turning top, eventually she

could not get dizzy inside the spin,

inside the little tornado's rhythm—

We want to be perpetual motion machines

but have to learn to turn the top

without tearing the world apart.

Funnel clouds ripped through the South each spring

and I wanted to take ballet

with my bad balance and spankings

for chewing gum in class (I had to spit

it out into that mean teacher's palm.

Why did she want that?)

What I saw in my head— what my body did—

told me I was good at not much.

I was good at sitting and standing still.

I was good at feeling hurt. I had no leverage.

The walls of a castle can be stormed from inside or out.

The expectations on both sides are serious

and those walls will eat you, eat you, EAT YOU!

Couldn't Say, and Didn't: Part 5

> I have a secret…If I can't tell it, I'll die, and if I do tell it, I'll not be allowed to live.
> — from the folktale "The King with the Horse's Ears"

In the Past the only way to see inside

was to cut the body open, but now

there can be a map of my whole brain, a universe

of cranial speckling, furrows there and back,

a thudding motor lower, a pulse through blood paths

and portals for what I don't need   to leave

and portals for what I might   to come in:

when you explain to me how sound

works I see wormholes

because really there is no place

that sound waves call home.

I wake from a dream in one house

as you fall asleep in another.

I'll never sleep again

in the house of my youth,

the same house of my mother's youth,

buried under another house now.

I'll go there and see if the big magnolia still stands.

I'll cut a slit into the bark

and tell the tree everything.

Couldn't Say, and Didn't: Part 6

I like to stare at the tips of trees, burn them into my eyes,
then place their ghosts against the sky in a private painting.

I like plants because they don't talk back.
With animals, it's always something or the other—

To be gentle:		walk on eggshells	(cut your feet).

To be elastic:		know the future		(live it anyway).

To be a martyr:		crave closeness		(deny yourself).

Last year I killed my dog and so far he has not come back to life.
He might be blowing around in the wind of an unknown field,
some woods I've never seen, the horizon of mankind
just visible in the distance.

Arriving later with music in your pocket I could hear you
through the door left cracked.
The sound of children playing carried over from a few streets away
when the wind was right.
I couldn't have avoided it if I'd wanted to.

Couldn't Say, and Didn't: Part 7

Ghost of a fin, the shine of scales

that drew you in, the song I ceased to sing.

Me of the sea, me of the air.

I could become Queen,

but the King will have to settle,

for now I only have these legs,

and I'm not even dizzy.

***

I didn't watch that movie you recommended

and I didn't finish your book.

I'm not making a very strong case for myself as a friend.

***

Plants *do* talk back.

They bitch & moan in yellow,

dry up the vine as a way of saying

less or *MORE*

***

What should we wear when the gods

disguise themselves in rags to test us?

I'll tell you a secret if you tell me one:

there is no compromise in Utopia.

Build a secret house under fireworks,

count the steps from Destiny to door.

Sacrifice the fruit that steals energy from the bloom,

fool the plant back into practice.

***

The King says we're not allowed

to say *I love you* too often, but Death says

to let the Queen do as she pleases.

A cold man remains cold unless shaken to his core.

***

The magnolia is gone.

No more boats will sail a concrete sea.

No other child will ever be me exactly.

Couldn't Say, and Didn't: Part 8

A rough winter, a stack of holidays

In this weather, birds come out to eat more if you throw seeds

Leave their tiny feet across the snow like twigs

The problem does not resolve

You do the littlest possible

You connect but don't connect

You love but you don't practice love

The tv sputters light

What is the color of mercy? Where is the romance?

Harness the energy of the line

Dismantle obligation

I love solidly   I wake up   I love intermittently

If you're hearing voices I'm hearing them too

Couldn't Say, and Didn't: Part 9

There's a buzzing somewhere in this room—
a cracked black thought,
a wasp at the window.

When I'm pulsing green around the edges
I know my soul doesn't live inside my body.
I am an astrological event:

> I wanted to be found and taken, claimed.
> Be a god, be a planet that knows its spin
> and never needs to sleep.

In truth, nothing is ours to keep,

no matter how much we buy it.

But if I learn that nearly nothing

is really a lot for you to say

then there is no place in this Universe I could be

where you would not be welcome.

Have I learned nothing at all?

The End of Change

I had a dream I was pressing my flat feet

into the ground so hard

trying not to stir up trouble,

trying not to float away.

A stone face in the sudden black,

all atmosphere removed,

sped through the void to reach me.

Breath rushed from its hard slit of a mouth

and I woke, and was in my own room again,

sitting up, tasked to tell the truth.

Do I control the lightning strike?

I will send it into our Tower.

I tried learning to read music—

a song in six, a song in five—

hid my skills with knives and strategy,

I listened and I played,

absorbed bad days and calmed fevers.

I learned to write the seals,

locate true names of what I wanted to bend.

I am not gathering angels or demons now,

just taking stock, counting the red things

running across the ground.

When it first began to happen,

I'd catch a thin glimpse

of something through the water

or something in the air.

36 dead birds littering the long bridge

across the salt bay

and everything I have loved falling into the sea.

The cluttered mess of a heart

that tries to copy the past

finds the bed is lumpy, full of sand,

and no one sleeps.

We are wearing our ghost suits.

There is so much dust.

At what point does the concrete vanish?

When does the sky give way to the celestial floor?

I'm spilling rubies from my mouth.

Red tulips are cups of blood,

the red smile is a flower.

Everything was red all along,

I just didn't see the warning.

Instead I chose to paint my walls that color.

Do what the sea god says—

the ocean wants to eat us and grind us into sand.

Why should I always be the one keeping

the peace between heaven and earth,

the only one climbing a ladder into the sky?

People come to me, asking to be fixed.

You need to come to me whole

but aware of your particles.

Roll yourself out like a scroll

through every planetary hour.

Let it not be your first time out of the alembic,

and let you not try to turn me into gold—

I can make my own.

If you agree, work alongside me.

Then I will be the fire and the fog—

whatever you need,

but I'm keeping my powers.

This Is What the Morning Is

if it is— it barely is, almost isn't— I'm almost but almost not here,
surprised at first light to be, still, or again, until the half-dead refrigerator
starts its whine and the rest of the aether dissipates. Solid now,
what I really want to do is go so far back down into the dark dream
I can't get back up and have to travel through the other side. I want
to find out what kind of world lies under this sleeping city, maybe
with trees growing from the ends of roots, spreading their own roots
into the edges of life as we know it to be. Maybe there is even air
down there, though probably no one needs to breathe. Sometimes at night
I'm almost there, but the panic of having   forces me back into my body.
Name for me one thing that doesn't wrinkle, doesn't bend. Everything will
with the right pressure. I am not so foolish that I don't know what isn't.
I just couldn't tell what you actually wanted. It was a rattlesnake waiting
anyway, some kind of rattlesnake business, thinking the path was clear
or that it was a path at all. Energy moves on either side of a moment,
but the moment itself is stale. Thank you for putting this desert into me.
There are some plants that will only flower there, lotuses of fire and air,
dream-things with yellow and white heaped-up crowns on the heads
of spiked May Queens, beastly children at play.

Index

abacus, 65
aether, 64, 67, 100, 104, 136
air, 13, 29, 33, 38, 44, 46, 48, 54, 56, 60, 66, 75, 77, 87, 96, 100, 107, 114, 116, 128, 133, 136.
  See also sea
alchemy, 26, 29, 34-35, 100-101, 106-107, 134-135
angel, 70, 89, 90, 94, 113
animals. *See indiv. types*
Annihilation. *See* movies
apple. *See* plant
architecture, 16, 29, 57, 58, 113.
  See also church; house
Aristotle, 75
art (and artists),
  Beardsley, Aubrey, 80-81
  Brueghel the Elder, Pieter, 43, 74
  Chihuly, Dale, 112
  De Chirico, Giorgio, 53-58
  Kandinsky, Wassily, 73
  Landscape with the Fall of Icarus, 74
  Mystery and Melancholy of a Street, 56
  Rothko, Mark, 120
  Salome with the Head of John the Baptist, 80
  Schiele, Egon, 62-63
  still life painting, 62
ash, 28, 29, 35, 109
babies. *See* children
Bactine, 102
ballet, 124
baseball cap, 54, 95
bed, 44, 63, 70, 96, 133
bees. *See* insects
bicycle, 32, 39, 82
bird(s), 31, 34, 43, 48-51, 67, 71, 94, 111, 130, 133
  crow, 46
  pigeon, 31, 57

vulture, 96
birth, 13, 56
birthday, 73, 74
blood, 16, 30, 67, 73, 120, 121, 126, 134
bloodroot, 120
boat, 53, 67, 116, 129
Bocca della Verità. *See* Mouth of Truth
body, 30, 31, 35, 38, 41, 72, 74-75, 93, 98, 116, 125, 126, 131, 136
bone, 26, 28, 30, 34, 38, 46, 62, 74, 110-112
bridge, 18, 46, 66, 112, 133
buttons, 43, 55, 114
castle, 18, 79, 125
cat, 96, 111
celestial realm, 40, 50, 71, 104, 134
cell division, 119
change, 50, 59, 67, 77
  transformation, 35, 60, 70, 118-119
Chernobyl, 32
children, 12, 18, 63, 111, 127
childhood, 12, 16, 18, 33, 124, 129
church, 54, 84
cathedral, 29
clairvoyance, 47, 96, 100, 132-133
cleaning, 52, 71, 80, 92
clouds, 81, 83, 84, 116, 124
coffee, 64, 65, 71
colors
  black, 17, 22, 36, 59, 100, 108, 120, 131, 132
  blue, 18, 20, 26, 35, 38, 47, 53, 73, 83
  golden, 49, 50, 54, 67, 104
  green, 18, 19, 49, 70, 71, 89, 92, 131
  grey, 26, 49, 100
  orange, 62

138

pink, 42, 66, 53, 73
red, 12, 26, 46, 54, 59, 83, 106, 107, 120, 133-134
white, 20, 34, 35, 37, 41, 59, 136
yellow, 49, 128, 136
comet, 71
comma, 117
confetti, 73
Cosmos. *See* celestial realm
creekbed, 102
crown, 136
cycles, 35
dance, 80
  card, 54
  floor, 73
day, 53, 55, 108, 110, 136
death, 15, 24-25, 31, 35, 61-63, 77, 82, 108, 113, 122, 123, 127, 129, 133
De Chirico, Giorgio. *See* art
demon, 133
devil, 120
dirt, 18, 33, 70, 120, 121
disappointment, 63, 114
dog, 32, 46, 82, 83, 127
door, 38, 38, 42, 47, 122, 127, 129
dream, 12, 47, 63, 72, 116, 118, 122, 126, 132, 136
Earth, 32, 40, 58, 74, 94, 101, 104, 134
electricity, 13, 38, 41, 55, 71, 94
elements, *See indiv. names*
endosymbiosis, 118
energy, 13, 118, 129, 130, 136. *See also* electricity
fairytale. *See* folktale
Fall, 104, 120
father, 16, 18, 32, 41, 47, 58, 100
fear, 62, 74-75, 83, 95-96, 118
fern. *See* plants
fever, 79, 132
fire, 13, 22-23, 29, 34, 59, 106, 107, 108, 135, 136
fireworks, 129

flowers. *See* plants
fog, 80, 115, 135
folktale, 77, 129
  King with the Horse's Ears, 126
  Little Mermaid, 124, 128
fox, 31, 32
fruit. *See* plant
fungi, 120
  mold, 20, 41, 110-111
game, 75, 77
gardening, 18-19, 44, 60-61, 83
Gemini, 48
ghost, 33, 44, 65, 67, 78, 86, 100, 127, 133
glass, 12, 14, 22, 34, 46, 56, 70, 110-115
grass, 49, 102
  blade whistle, 12, 97, 106-107
  St. Augustine, 12
grief, 48, 62, 65, 74, 120
hair, 43, 67, 91, 111, 116, 123
hands, 16, 18, 27, 39, 58, 63, 64, 67, 83, 85, 88, 90, 91, 93, 94, 100, 120, 122
heart, 78, 111, 112, 126, 133
hoarding, 30, 63
holidays, 130
horse, 58, 102-105
  sawhorse, 16
house, 30, 32, 38, 40, 41, 43, 46-47, 59, 65, 92, 98, 103, 110, 115, 123, 126, 129
hydra, 111
Icarus, 74
ice, 13, 29, 41, 42, 43, 76, 78, 111, 112
Icees, coke, 49
infinity, 39, 59
insects, 19, 65, 67, 70, 73, 100, 120, 123, 131
  ants, 19, 20, 31, 32,
  bees, 100-101
  flies, 41, 65, 66, 73
  lightning bugs, 12

139

island, 117
Kandinsky, Wassily. *See* art
king, 77, 126, 128, 129
labyrinth, 74
ladder, 134
ley lines, 67
light(s), 13, 35, 41, 55, 64, 66, 71, 73, 84, 100, 108, 110, 111, 120, 130, 136
lightning. *See* weather
Landscape with the Fall of Icarus. *See* art
Lifesavers, 71
Little Mermaid, the. *See* folktales
loss, 12, 13, 74, 96, 98
love, 50, 54, 58, 60-66, 78, 80, 118, 129, 130
mac & cheese, 62
machine, 31, 32, 33, 34, 65, 121, 124
magic, 29, 64, 67, 78, 80
  classical elements. *See indiv. names*
  planetary magic, 134
  ritual, 44
  sigil, 65
magnification, 12, 41, 70, 91, 111
map, 33, 82, 126
maze, 74
memory, 26, 35, 67, 83, 111, 116
Mercury,
  element, 48, 107
  god, 107
  planet, 38, 74
metal, 28, 40, 71, 94
meteor, 74
Minotaur, 74
mirror, 22
misery. *See* grief
mold. *See* fungi
moon (the), 40, 55, 64-65, 95, 100, 103, 117
mother, 18, 59, 73, 100, 102, 126
mountain, 104, 108
Mouth of Truth, 132
movies, 54, 128

Annihilation, 118-119
museum, 104, 110
music, 16, 29, 42, 96-97, 106, 127, 132
nemesis, 123
night, 36, 40, 42, 52, 53, 54, 55, 59, 63, 72, 83, 86, 96, 100, 103, 104, 110, 117, 120, 136
nightmare. *See* dream
nostalgia, 62
object, 12, 63, 65, 67, 97, 121
ocean. *See* sea
panic, 136
path, 50, 71, 76, 78, 101, 126, 136
patterns, 12, 45, 73, 105
  china pattern, 12, 14, 36
philosophy, 75, 103
phone, 96, 120
physics, 75, 126
planets, 39, 41, 131. *See also* celestial realm; planetary magic; *indiv. names*
plants, 12, 17-19, 22, 70, 127, 128
  chloroplasts, 118
  fern, 13, 19, 70
  flowers, 18-19, 32, 41, 47, 52, 55, 58, 59, 60-61, 72, 81, 120, 136
  fruit, 17, 20-21, 34, 66, 73, 120
  seeds, 17, 19, 44, 55, 60-61, 63, 130
  trees, 32, 42, 43, 50, 65, 73, 76, 80, 98, 114, 127
  talk to, 126
  turning into, 119
Pliny the Younger, 108
Pluto, 104
practice, 78, 103, 130
promise(s), 13, 54, 55, 56, 62
queen(s), 77-78, 128, 129, 136
rabbit, 96
rain. *See* weather
rattlesnake. *See* snake
reaching (gesture), 36, 38, 60, 88, 108, 120
redemption, 58

refrigerator, 55, 136
resurrection, 32, 64
Rilke, Rainer Maria, 84
ritual. *See* magic
roads, 12, 13, 17, 46, 49-51, 76, 121
rock, 32, 40, 41, 59, 83, 90, 104, 106, 107, 124, 132
roots, 32-33, 41, 49, 82, 98, 100, 117, 136
Rothko, Mark. *See* art
rules, 14, 75, 77
sacrifice, 59, 129
saint 56
  Saint Clare 86-94
  Saint Francis of Assisi 86-94
  Saint John the Baptist, 80-81
salamander, 118
Salome, 80-81
salt, 66, 124, 107, 116, 133
sand, 18, 28, 34, 48, 76, 133, 134
  dunes, 71, 76
sap, 111, 114
Schiele, Egon. *See* art
scissors. *See* tools
sea, 18, 28, 37, 49, 71, 74, 128, 133
  sea air, 48, 121
sea monkeys, 70
seasons, 19, 71. *See also indiv. names*
secrets, 13, 47, 52, 56, 119, 126, 129
shadow, 22, 41, 47, 49, 56, 65, 79, 100
shoes, 20, 36, 43, 49, 55, 95, 120
sigil. *See* magic
signs, 45, 46-47, 132-134
silence, 41, 57, 66
singing. *See* music
sky, 38, 53, 55, 74, 81, 83, 98, 104, 108, 116, 127, 134
sleep, 24, 36, 41, 48, 63, 72, 81, 91, 95, 103, 117, 126, 131, 132, 133, 136
smoke, 55, 95, 109
snake, 17, 136
  rattlesnake, 136

snow. *See* weather
solitude, 12-13, 20, 38-39, 42, 52, 54, 59, 62, 98
sorrow. *See* grief
sound, 31, 32, 41, 49, 54, 55, 72, 78, 85, 96, 127. *See also* music; voice(s)
  waves, 126
Spring, 48, 66, 76, 124
spores, 70, 110
stars, 35, 58, 109
still life painting. *See* art
stone. *See* rock
storm. *See* weather
sugar, 20, 28, 65, 118
Summer, 17, 49
sun (the), 41, 55, 60, 67, 74, 100, 116, 117, 119
symbiosis, 118
Tarot, 118
  Knight of Cups, the, 60
  Magician, the, 106-107
  Tower, the, 79, 132
taxidermy, 30-31
tea, 26-28, 34, 95
  cup, 14, 20, 26-27, 32, 30, 71, 84
teeth, 24, 25, 55, 65, 67, 71, 100
television. *See* tv
thresholds, 75, 100
time, 12, 36, 72, 76, 84, 101, 102-103, 106, 120
  timing, 64, 66, 83
tools, 16, 38, 56, 73, 85, 106-107, 136
  scissors, 22, 73, 85, 91
top, 124
tornado, 124
transformation. *See* change
tree. *See* plants
tv, 63, 130
Utopia, 129
vehicles, 52, 104
  car, 13, 44, 17, 18, 32, 64, 66
  train, 27, 40, 53

veil(s), 80, 97
vessel, 75, 92
voice(s), 18, 20, 42, 90, 108, 130
volcano, 108-109
waiting, 12, 41, 45, 123, 136
water, 13, 18, 21, 29, 30, 41, 44, 48,
    52, 60, 73, 75, 81, 82, 103, 107,
    112-113, 133
weather, 45, 77, 104, 130
  lightning, 13, 38, 86, 132
  rain, 12-13, 62, 67, 80, 81, 104, 110
  snow, 29, 41, 76, 78, 98, 130
  storm, 12, 18, 83
  wind, 44, 46, 116, 127
window, 17, 22, 39, 47, 53, 66, 67,
    71, 86, 100, 108, 113, 114, 131
wings, 31, 34, 74, 96
winter, 38, 41, 66, 76, 87, 98, 102,
    111, 130. *See also* weather
woods. *See* trees
wormholes, 126

Acknowledgements/Notes

The Accidental Rarefication of Pattern #5609 appears courtesy of bedouin books, its original publisher in 2012.

Thank you to the following journals and anthologies in which some of these poems (in these or other versions) first appeared: *Bodyprint: An Anthology of the Body, Cirque, Eratio, Fireweed, Gobshite Quarterly, Gramma, Hawaii Review, Louisiana Literature, Mid-American Review, Osiris, The Portable Boog Reader, Quaranzine, Susan, Thraca, Toy Poems*, and *The Zymoglyphic Anthology, Volume II.*

Thanks to the Independent Publishing Resource Center in Portland, OR, and Sou'Wester Arts in Seaview, WA, for providing retreats that encouraged the creation of a number of these poems.

A special thank you to Liz Mehl, Justin Rigamonti, and everyone at Poetry Press Week, as well as my team of collaborators in late 2014 (Sierra Bittinger, Gretchen Lohry-Smith, Brandi Katherine Herrera, Katharina Raven, Aspen Farer, Hannah Palcic, and Julie Verdini). The series "Couldn't Say, and Didn't" began as part of that performance.

Thank you to writer Shayla Lawson for including me in your Pick-a-Thon Spoken lineup in 2017 where some of these poems were debuted and I had the chance to perform on the same stage that Dinosaur Jr. played on later that night, thus fulfilling in convoluted fashion one of my childhood fantasies.

"Hunters," "I Only Wanted You for Your Warmth," and "The Tilting Horizon Over the World Full of Holes" are part of The Doppelgänger Museum, a collaboration with visual artist Aspen Farer.

"I Am Nothing's Mother" exists as part of a text and image project with visual artist Noelle Barce in which she and I both illustrated the poem, section by section. It was shown at the Walters Cultural Arts Center in Hillsboro, Oregon, in 2019.

"A Sudden Swerve" was inspired by a "poem scaffold" created by the poet Emily Kendal Frey. "It Takes Me by Surprise" was crafted using an exercise in Richard Hugo's *The Triggering Town.*

The titles "The Enigma of Arrival" and "Mystery and Melancholy of a Street" are borrowed/adapted from paintings by Giorgio de Chirico. "Everything Is Red" retroactively owes a debt to James Galvin's poem "Untitled, 1968," also about Mark Rothko and his use of this color. The phrase "nourished by the mere elements" in one of the St. Clare poem titles is borrowed from the book *Possession* by A.S. Byatt. Lines in "The End of Change" ("Red tulips are cups of blood,/the red smile is a flower") are inspired by a passage in Margaret Atwood's *The Handmaid's Tale* ("The tulips are not tulips of blood, the red smiles are not flowers, neither thing makes a comment on the other.") "Cannot Be Sustained" references the 2018 film *Annihilation*. "The Light and the Clouds Came In" references the Rainer Maria Rilke poem "Archaic Torso of Apollo": "...for here there is no place/that does not see you, You must change your life."

Thanks to Stephanie Adams-Santos, Sarah Bartlett, Michelle Ruiz Keil, and Paul Maziar for reading these so thoroughly in advance of publication and for being inspirations with your own creative work. Thanks to Lucy Volker for your stunning artwork on the cover (see more of her work at www.luciavolker.com), to Hannah Piper Burns for consulting with the stars, and to Nation William Crow for your fabric translations and for helping me realize the scale of sleep. And final thanks to the team at Deep Overstock for the chance to publish this book in the exact form I had envisioned.

Coleman Stevenson is the author of *Breakfast: 43 Poems* (Reprobate/GobQ Books, 2015), *The Accidental Rarefication of Pattern #5609* (Bedouin Books, 2012), *The Dark Exact Tarot Guide*, and a book of essays accompanying the card game *Metaphysik*. Her writing has also appeared in a variety of journals and anthologies, and she is a regular contributor for tarot.com. In addition to her work as a designer of tarot and oracle decks through her company The Dark Exact, her fine art work, exhibited in galleries around the Pacific Northwest, focuses on the intersections between image and text. She has been a guest curator for various gallery spaces in the Portland, Oregon, area, and has taught poetry, design theory, and cultural studies at a number of different institutions there, most currently for the Literary Arts Delve series, which includes seminars at the Portland Art Museum.
http://www.colemanstevenson.com/

www.ingramcontent.com/pod-product-compliance
Lightning Source LLC
Chambersburg PA
CBHW030332100526
44592CB00010B/669